MW00568749

Anxiety disorders

An information guide

Neil A. Rector, PhD
Danielle Bourdeau, MD
Kate Kitchen, MSW
Linda Joseph-Massiah, RN, PhD
Judith M. Laposa, PhD

Centre for Addiction and Mental Health

A Pan American Health Organization /
World Health Organization Collaborating Centre

Library and Archives Canada Cataloging in Publication

Rector, Neil A., author
    Anxiety disorders : an information guide / Neil A. Rector, PhD, Danielle Bour-
deau, MD, Kate Kitchen, MSW, Linda Joseph-Massiah, PhD, and Judith Laposa,
PhD. -- Revised edition.

Revision of: Anxiety disorders, an information guide. Toronto: Centre for Addiction
and Mental Health, 2005.
Includes bibliographical references.
Issued in print and electronic formats.
ISBN 978-1-77114-337-0 (PAPERBACK). -- ISBN 978-1-77114-338-7 (PDF). -- ISBN 978-
1-77114-339-4 (HTML). -- ISBN 978-1-77114-340-0 (EPUB). -- ISBN 978-1-77114-341-7
(KINDLE)

    1. Anxiety disorders--Popular works. 2. Anxiety--Popular works. 3. Anxiety
disorders--Patients--Family relationships. I. Laposa, Judith Megan, 1976-, author II.
Kitchen, Kate, author III. Bourdeau, Danielle , author IV. Joseph-Massiah, Linda,
author V. Centre for Addiction and Mental Health, issuing body VI. Title.

RC531.R42 2016   616.85'22   C2016-903234-5
                                                         C2016-903235-3

Printed in Canada

This publication may be available in other formats. For information about alternative
formats or other CAMH publications, or to place an order, please contact CAMH
Publications:
Toll-free: 1 800 661-1111
Toronto: 416 595-6059
E-mail: publications@camh.ca
Online store: http://store.camh.ca
Website: www.camh.ca

Disponible en français sous le titre :
Les troubles anxieux : Guide d'Information

This guide was produced by CAMH Education

3973b / 08-2016 / PM121

Contents

Acknowledgments

We thank the people who shared their personal experiences with anxiety with us, and the people with anxiety disorders, family members and mental health professionals who reviewed earlier drafts. Reviewers included Sheila Gamblen and Veronica King; professional reviewers were Sandie Leith, MSW, RSW, Mary Lalonde, OT, Donna Weick, MSW, RSW, and Neely Bakshi, MD.

We would also like to thank past authors of other guides in this series whose work provided a foundation for the information presented here. In particular, we would like to thank Christina Bartha, Carol Parker and Cathy Thomson.

Introduction

This guide is for people with anxiety disorders, their families, partners, friends and anyone else who might be interested.

The many aspects of anxiety disorders discussed in this book will answer some common questions, and help readers discuss anxiety disorders with treatment providers.

1 Anxiety and anxiety disorders

Everyone feels anxiety from time to time. Few people get through a week without some anxious tension or a feeling that something is not going to go well. We may feel anxiety when we're facing an important event, such as an exam or job interview, or when we perceive some threat or danger, such as waking to strange sounds in the night. However, such everyday anxiety is generally occasional, mild and brief, while the anxiety felt by the person with an anxiety disorder occurs frequently, is more intense, and lasts longer—up to hours, or even days.

Unfortunately, anxiety disorders are common. Research shows that up to one in four adults has an anxiety disorder sometime in their life, and that one person in 10 is likely to have had an anxiety disorder in the past year. Anxiety disorders are the most common mental health problem in women, and are second only to substance use disorders in men. Anxiety disorders can make it hard for people to work or study, to manage daily tasks and to relate well with others, and often result in financial strain and profound personal suffering.

People often live with anxiety disorders for years before they are diagnosed and treated. If you suspect that you have an anxiety disorder, it is important to seek professional treatment as soon as possible. Anxiety disorders are treatable, and early treatment can help to ensure treatment success.

The main categories of anxiety disorders are *specific phobias, panic disorder, agoraphobia, generalized anxiety disorder, social anxiety disorder, selective mutism* and *separation anxiety disorder* (American Psychiatric Association [APA], 2013).

Each of these anxiety disorders is distinct in some ways, but they all share the same hallmark features:

· irrational and excessive fear
· apprehensive and tense feelings
· difficulty managing daily tasks and/or distress related to these tasks.

In the following examples, Susan and John* show these common features, although the precise nature of their fears differ.

Susan has had recurrent and unexpected panic attacks for the past five years:

> *It started on a night when I was driving home in the rain. I began to feel shaky and dizzy, and had trouble focusing. At first, I thought it was something that I had eaten earlier, but then my mind started to drift, and I thought, "What if I pass out?" and "What if I'm dying?" I started to shake all over, and it was as if my entire body was wired. I quickly pulled the car over and called my daughter to come and get me. Since then, I've had dozens and dozens of these attacks. At first, the attacks occurred just when I was driving, but now I experience them in shopping malls, standing in line-ups and even on the bus. It seems as if I spend most of my day worrying and waiting for the next attack.*

---

* All names and identifying details have been changed.

John describes a lifelong pattern of being excessively shy and fearing embarrassment in social situations:

> *For as long as I can remember, and as far back as when I was seven years old, I hated being the centre of attention. In class, I tried to remain as invisible as possible, praying that the teacher would not call upon me to answer a question. When it was my turn to make presentations, I wouldn't sleep for a week, worrying that I would forget what I was supposed to say, stumble over my words, and look completely stupid. It's as if nothing's changed: now at work I dread having to attend meetings, meet with the boss, have lunch with colleagues, and the worst, give monthly reports to the team. I'm pretty sure everyone knows how uncomfortable I am, and they all probably think I look weird and sound stupid.*

To better understand the nature of anxiety disorders such as those experienced by Susan and John, we need to first explore the nature of "normal" anxiety. Later in this chapter, we'll describe the key fears and components of each major anxiety disorder.

What is normal anxiety?

A certain amount of anxiety is normal and necessary; it can lead you to act on your concerns and protect you from harm. In some situations, anxiety can even be essential to your survival. If you were standing at the edge of a curb, for example, and a car swerved toward you, you would immediately perceive danger, feel alarm and jump back to avoid the car. This normal anxiety response, called the "fight or flight" response, is what prompts you to either fight or flee from danger.

When we feel danger, or think that danger is about to occur, the brain sends a message to the nervous system, which responds by releasing adrenaline. Increased adrenaline causes us to feel alert and energetic, and gives us a spurt of strength, preparing us to attack (fight) or escape to safety (flight). Increased adrenaline can also have unpleasant side-effects. These can include feeling nervous, tense, dizzy, sweaty, shaky or breathless. Such effects can be disturbing, but they are not harmful to the body and generally do not last long.

How does anxiety affect us?

Whenever the fight or flight response is activated by danger, either real or imagined, it leads to changes in three "systems of functioning": the way you think (cognitive), the way your body feels and works (physical), and the way you act (behavioural). How much these three systems change varies, depending on the person and the context.

- **Cognitive:** Attention shifts immediately and automatically to the potential threat. The effect on a person's thinking can range from mild worry to extreme terror.
- **Physical:** Effects include heart palpitations or increased heart rate, shallow breathing, trembling or shaking, sweating, dizziness or lightheadedness, feeling "weak in the knees," freezing, muscle tension, shortness of breath and nausea.
- **Behavioural:** People engage in certain behaviours and refrain from others as a way to protect themselves from anxiety (e.g., taking self-defence classes or avoiding certain streets after dark).

It is important to recognize that the cognitive, physical and behavioural response systems of anxiety often change together. For instance, if you are spending a lot of time worrying about your finances (cognitive), you are likely to feel physically on edge and nervous (physical), and may spend quite a bit of time checking your household budget and investments (behavioural). Or if you're preparing for an important exam, you may worry about doing your best (cognitive), feel tense and maybe even have "butterflies" (physical), and initially avoid studying and then cram at the last minute (behavioural).

The key points to remember about anxiety are that it is:
· *normal* and experienced by every living organism
· *necessary* for survival and adaptation
· *not harmful or dangerous*
· typically *short-lived*
· sometimes *useful* for performance (at low or moderate levels).

When is anxiety a problem?

Everyone experiences symptoms of anxiety, but they are generally occasional and short-lived, and do not cause problems. But when the cognitive, physical and behavioural symptoms of anxiety are persistent and severe, and anxiety causes distress in a person's life to the point that it negatively affects his or her ability to work or study, socialize and manage daily tasks, it may be beyond normal range.

The following examples of anxiety symptoms may indicate an anxiety disorder:
· **Cognitive:** *anxious thoughts* (e.g., "I'm losing control"), *anxious predictions* (e.g., "I'm going to fumble my words and humiliate myself") and *anxious beliefs* (e.g., "Only weak people get anxious").
· **Physical:** *excessive physical reactions relative to the context* (e.g., heart racing and feeling short of breath in response to being at

the mall). The physical symptoms of anxiety may be mistaken for symptoms of a physical illness, such as a heart attack.

· **Behavioural**: *avoidance of feared situations* (e.g., driving), *avoidance of activities that elicit sensations similar to those experienced when anxious* (e.g., exercise), *subtle avoidances* (behaviours that aim to distract the person, e.g., talking more during periods of anxiety) and *safety behaviours* (habits to minimize anxiety and feel "safer," e.g., always having a cell phone on hand to call for help).

Several factors determine whether the anxiety warrants the attention of mental health professionals, including:
· the *degree* of distress caused by the anxiety symptoms
· the *level of effect* the anxiety symptoms have on a person's ability to work or study, socialize and manage daily tasks
· the *context* in which the anxiety occurs.

What are the anxiety disorders?

An anxiety disorder may make people feel anxious most of the time or for brief intense episodes, which may occur for no apparent reason. People with anxiety disorders may have anxious feelings that are so uncomfortable that they avoid daily routines and activities that might cause these feelings. Some people have occasional anxiety attacks so intense that they are terrified or immobilized. People with anxiety disorders are usually aware of the irrational and excessive nature of their fears. When they come for treatment, many say, "I know my fears are unreasonable, but I just can't seem to stop them."

The major categories of anxiety disorders are classified according to the focus of the anxiety. A brief description of each is given below, based on the diagnostic criteria outlined in the *Diagnostic and*

Statistical Manual of Mental Disorders (DSM-5; APA, 2013). Although each anxiety disorder can have many different symptoms, one representative example has been chosen to illustrate the typical cognitive, physical and behavioural symptoms of each disorder.

RECENT CHANGES IN WHAT IS CLASSIFIED AS AN ANXIETY DISORDER

In 2013, the DSM-5 replaced the DSM-IV. In the DSM-5, obsessive-compulsive disorder (OCD), agoraphobia without a history of panic disorder, acute stress disorder and posttraumatic stress disorder (PTSD) are no longer classified as anxiety disorders, as they were in DSM-IV. OCD is now found in the obsessive-compulsive and related disorders category, and PTSD and acute stress disorder are now found under the trauma and stressor-related disorders category. New additions to the anxiety disorder category include separation anxiety disorder and selective mutism.

PANIC DISORDER

Description
· Panic disorder involves recurrent, unexpected panic attacks (e.g., heart palpitations, sweating, trembling) followed by at least one month of
  a. persistent concern about having another panic attack or the consequences of a panic attack (e.g., having a heart attack), and/or
  b. significant behaviour changes related to the attacks (e.g., avoiding exercise or places for fear of having a panic attack) (APA, 2013).
· Panic attacks may be accompanied by agoraphobia (see next category of anxiety disorder below).

Examples of symptoms
COGNITIVE
· "I'm having a heart attack."
· "I'm suffocating."

PHYSICAL
· accelerated heart rate
· chest pain or discomfort
· dizziness, nausea
· trembling or shaking
· shortness of breath

BEHAVIOURAL
· avoidance of places where the person had anxiety symptoms in the past (e.g., a certain grocery store) or similar places (e.g., all grocery stores)
· avoidance of travel, crowds, line-ups
· avoidance of strenuous activities (e.g., exercise)

AGORAPHOBIA

Description
· Agoraphobia involves marked anxiety for at least six months, in at least two of the following five situations: *using public transportation, being in open spaces, being in enclosed places, standing in line or being in a crowd,* and *being away from home alone.* People with agoraphobia avoid these situations, or endure them with distress. The main concern in these situations is that it would be hard to escape, or that others would not be able to help if the person had panic symptoms (APA, 2013).

Examples of symptoms
COGNITIVE
- "I'm going to be trapped."
- "No one will be able to help me."

PHYSICAL
- accelerated heart rate
- shortness of breath

BEHAVIOURAL
- avoidance of public transportation, open spaces, enclosed places, being out of the house alone, standing in lines and/or being in crowds
- requiring the presence of a companion in situations or places related to the anxiety

SPECIFIC PHOBIA

Description
- A specific phobia involves a "marked fear or anxiety about a specific object or situation" (APA, 2013, p. 197).
- There are five subtypes of specific phobia: *animal type*, such as fear of mice or spiders; *natural environment type*, such as fear of storms or heights; *blood-injection-injury* type, such as fear of seeing blood or receiving an injection; *situational type*, such as fear of public transportation, elevators or enclosed spaces; and *other type*, such as fear of choking or vomiting.

Examples of symptoms
COGNITIVE
- "This plane will crash."
- "The dog will bite me."

PHYSICAL
· sweating
· muscle tension
· dizziness

BEHAVIOURAL
· avoidance of air travel
· need to escape

SOCIAL ANXIETY DISORDER

Description
· Social anxiety disorder (also known as social phobia) involves a "marked fear or anxiety about social situations in which the person may be exposed to possible scrutiny by others" (APA, 2013, p. 202). This fear and/or avoidance related to social situations lasts at least six months.
· Fears might be associated with most social situations related to public performance or social interactions, such as participating in small groups, meeting strangers, dating or playing sports.

Examples of symptoms
COGNITIVE
· "I'll look anxious and stupid."
· "People will think I'm weird."

PHYSICAL
· blushing
· sweating
· dry mouth

BEHAVIOURAL
· avoidance of social gatherings, parties, meetings
· avoidance of public speaking

GENERALIZED ANXIETY DISORDER

Description
- Generalized anxiety disorder (GAD) involves "excessive anxiety and worry, occurring more days than not for at least six months, about a number of events or activities (such as work or school performance)" (APA, 2013, p. 222).
- GAD is characterized by difficulty in controlling worry and at least three associated physical symptoms (e.g., muscle tension, sleep difficulties, trouble concentrating).

Examples of symptoms
COGNITIVE
- "Something's going to go wrong."
- "This worry is going to make me nuts."
- "I need to be sure nothing bad is going to happen."

PHYSICAL
- muscle tension
- feeling keyed up or on edge
- restlessness, irritability
- sleep disturbance

BEHAVIOURAL
- avoidance of news, newspapers
- restricted activities due to excessive worries about what could happen
- excessive reassurance seeking or over-preparing

SEPARATION ANXIETY DISORDER

Description
- Separation anxiety disorder involves excessive fear and/or anxiety about being separated from home or from a person or people to

whom one is attached.
· The level of fear is not appropriate to the person's age or development.
· The fear, anxiety or avoidance occurs for at least one month in children or adolescents, and at least six months in adults (APA, 2013).

Examples of symptoms
COGNITIVE
· "Something bad will happen to person X if I am not around him/her."
· "Some event (e.g., getting lost or sick) will take me away from person X."

PHYSICAL
· headache
· stomach ache
· vomiting

BEHAVIOURAL
· reluctance or refusal to go out, for fear of separation
· avoidance of being alone or without person X
· refusal to sleep if person X is not nearby

SELECTIVE MUTISM

Description
· Selective mutism involves consistently not speaking "in specific situations where there is an expectation for speaking (e.g., at school), despite speaking in other situations" (APA, p 195).
· It occurs for at least a month (longer than a month if the first month of school) and often interferes with academic achievement.
· It often co-exists with shyness and/or social phobia.

Examples of symptoms
COGNiTIVE
· "I wish school was shorter."
· "What will they think of me?"

PHYSICAL
· stomach ache
· racing heart
· shortness of breath

BEHAVIOURAL
· not speaking in many social situations
· speaking only in the presence of immediate family
· refusing to go to school
· difficulty making eye contact

Although obsessive-compulsive disorder, acute stress disorder and posttraumatic stress disorder are no longer classified as anxiety disorders, the information provided here on cognitive-behavioural therapy, recovery, relapse prevention and considerations for families still applies to these diagnoses.

2 What causes anxiety disorders?

There are no clear-cut answers as to why some people develop an anxiety disorder, although research suggests that a number of factors may be involved. Like most mental health problems, anxiety disorders appear to be caused by a combination of biological factors, psychological factors and challenging life experiences, including:
· stressful or traumatic life events
· a family history of anxiety disorders
· childhood development issues
· alcohol, medications or illegal substances
· other medical or psychiatric problems.

Psychological factors

The two main schools of thought that attempt to explain the psychological influences on anxiety disorders are the *cognitive* and *behavioural* theories. The ideas expressed by these theories help us to understand cognitive-behavioural treatment, which will be outlined in the next chapter. A third way of looking at the psychological causes of anxiety is the *developmental* theory, which seeks to understand our experience of anxiety as adults by looking at what we learn as children.

COGNITIVE THEORY

Danger is a part of life. To protect us, evolution has genetically prepared us to fear danger. We know to avoid vicious animals and to be careful at great heights. Cognitive theory suggests, however, that people with anxiety disorders are prone to *overestimate* danger and its potential consequences. For example, people may overestimate the danger of particular animals, such as spiders or snakes, and thus believe that harm from that animal is far greater and more common than it actually is. Thinking of the worst possible scenario, they may imagine that a snake will bite and poison them, when it may be completely harmless. This is known as *catastrophizing*, and is common among people with anxiety disorders.

People who overestimate danger tend to avoid situations that might expose them to what they fear. For example, a person who fears flying will avoid trips that require air travel. Such behaviours are referred to as *safety behaviours* because they momentarily allow a person to feel less anxiety. However, when feared situations are avoided, the fears are strengthened. Cognitive theory suggests that fears can be reduced when people are able to experience the thing that they fear, allowing them to see that it is not as dangerous as they once believed.

BEHAVIOURAL THEORY

Behavioural theory suggests that people learn to associate the fear felt during a stressful or traumatic life event with certain cues, such as a place, a sound or a feeling. When the cues reoccur, they cause the fear to be re-experienced. Once the association between the fear and the cue is learned, it is automatic, immediate and out of conscious control. The fear is felt before there is time to tell if danger is near. Such cues may be *external* or *internal*.

An example of an external cue might be a certain smell that occurred at the time of the stressful event. When this smell occurs again, even at a time when there is no danger present, the person is reminded of the event and becomes fearful. Internal cues, such as a rapid heart rate, may also provoke fear if the person's heart raced during the actual threat. Later, when the person's heart beats rapidly during a workout routine, he or she may become fearful.

People with anxiety disorders may go to extreme lengths to avoid such cues. The original cues may even generalize to other similar cues, such as a bad encounter with a bulldog leading to the avoidance of all dogs. When people avoid such cues, they may feel more secure, but in the long run, these avoidance behaviours actually increase the anxiety associated with the cues. Avoidance prevents the person from "unlearning" the association, which can only be done when the person is exposed to such cues in a safe situation.

Developmental theory

According to developmental theory, the way in which children learn to predict and interpret life events contributes to the amount of anxiety they experience later in life. The amount of control people feel over their own lives is strongly related to the amount of anxiety they experience. A person's sense of control can range from confidence that whatever happens is entirely in his or her hands, to feeling complete uncertainty and helplessness over upcoming life events. People who feel that life is out of their control are likely to feel more fear and anxiety. For example, these people may feel that no amount of preparation or qualifications will give them any control over the outcome of an upcoming job interview, and they arrive at the interview fearing rejection.

Biological factors

The biological causes and effects of anxiety disorders include problems with brain chemistry and brain activity; genetics; and medical, psychiatric and substance use issues.

REGULATION OF BRAIN CHEMISTRY

Research has revealed a link between anxiety and problems with the regulation of various *neurotransmitters*—the brain's chemical messengers that transmit signals between brain cells. Three major neurotransmitters are involved in anxiety: serotonin, norepinephrine and gamma-aminobutyric acid (GABA).

Serotonin

Serotonin plays a role in the regulation of mood, aggression, impulses, sleep, appetite, body temperature and pain. A number of medications used to treat anxiety disorders raise the level of serotonin available to transmit messages.

Norepinephrine

Norepinephrine is involved in the fight or flight response and in the regulation of sleep, mood and blood pressure. Acute stress increases the release of norepinephrine. In people with anxiety disorders, especially those with panic disorder, the system controlling the release of norepinephrine appears to be poorly regulated. Some medications help to stabilize the amount of norepinephrine available to transmit messages.

GABA

GABA plays a role in helping to induce relaxation and sleep, and in preventing overexcitation. Medications known as *benzodiazepines* enhance the activity of GABA, producing a calming effect.

CHANGES IN BRAIN ACTIVITY

Modern brain-imaging techniques have allowed researchers to study the activity of specific areas of the brain in people with anxiety disorders. Such studies have found, for example:

- abnormalities in cerebral blood flow and metabolism, and also structural anomalies (e.g., atrophy) in the *frontal, occipital* and *temporal* lobes of the brain
- that serotonin, norepinephrine and GABA activity in the *limbic system*, which controls memory and anxiety and fear responses, is most likely responsible for anxiety about the future
- that activity in the *locus ceruleus* (with a high number of norepinephrine neurons) and the *median raphe nucleus* (with a high number of serotonin neurons) appears to be involved in the production of panic attacks
- that activity in the *norepinephrine* systems in the body and the brain produces physical symptoms of anxiety, such as blushing, sweating and palpitations, which may cause people to become alarmed; these systems have also been linked to the production of flashbacks in people with posttraumatic stress disorder.

GENETIC FACTORS

Research confirms that genetic factors play a role in the development of anxiety disorders. People are more likely to have an anxiety disorder if they have a relative who also has an anxiety disorder.

MEDICAL FACTORS

Alcohol, medications and illegal substances

Substance use may induce anxiety symptoms, either while the person is intoxicated or when the person is in withdrawal. The substances most often associated with generalized anxiety or panic symptoms are stimulants, including caffeine, illegal drugs such as cocaine, and prescription drugs such as methylphenidate (e.g., Ritalin).

Medical conditions

A range of medical conditions can cause anxiety symptoms and result in anxiety disorders. For example, both panic and generalized anxiety symptoms can result from medical conditions, especially those of the glands, heart, lungs or brain. Most often, treatment of the medical condition reduces symptoms of anxiety.

Psychiatric conditions

People with other psychiatric disorders often also have symptoms of anxiety. Sometimes it is the symptoms of the other disorder, such as depression or psychosis, that heighten a person's anxiety.

In such cases the person may not be diagnosed as having an anxiety disorder.

People who are diagnosed with anxiety disorders may also have other psychiatric disorders; most often, these are other types of anxiety disorders, or substance use disorders or depression.

Two out of three people with panic disorder will have a major depressive episode at some point in their lifetime. When depression occurs in someone with an anxiety disorder, it is of particular concern since these two problems in combination increase the person's risk for suicide. Most often, the anxiety disorder comes first, and as the impairment due to the anxiety disorder increases, depression sets in also. Importantly, there are well established and effective treatments for both anxiety and depressive disorders.

Other factors

Studies show that people who are anxious tend to have an irregular pattern of breathing, alternating from hyperventilation to holding their breath. This pattern of breathing contributes to further symptoms (e.g., lightheadedness, dizziness and possibly fainting) and increases the feelings of anxiety.

3 Treatments for anxiety disorders

Experts agree that the most effective form of psychological treatment for the anxiety disorders is disorder-specific cognitive-behavioural therapy (CBT). Medications have also been proven effective, and many people receive CBT and medication in combination.

Cognitive-behavioural therapy

CBT is a brief, problem-focused approach to treatment based on the cognitive and behavioural aspects of anxiety disorders.

Typically, CBT consists of 12 to 15 weekly one-hour sessions if you are working one on one with a therapist, or two-hour sessions if the treatment is in a group setting. In the initial sessions, the person with the anxiety disorder works with the therapist to understand the person's problems. The person's symptoms of anxiety are assessed within a cognitive-behavioural framework, and the goals and tasks of therapy are established. As the therapy progresses, behavioural and cognitive tasks are assigned to help the person with the anxiety disorder learn skills to reduce anxiety symptoms. As the symptoms improve, the therapist also focuses on underlying issues that may pose a risk for *relapse*, a term used to describe the return of symptoms.

Homework assignments between sessions can include facing a feared situation alone, recording thoughts and feelings in different anxiety-provoking situations, or reading relevant material.

Following treatment, therapists often schedule less frequent "booster" sessions.

WHAT DOES CBT INVOLVE?

A standard component of CBT treatment is *exposure therapy*, which involves gradually exposing the person, either directly or through the person's imagination, to his or her feared situation that triggers anxiety. For instance, the person who fears dogs will be asked to spend time with dogs, the person who has panic attacks in the mall will be requested to go to malls, and the person who fears embarrassing himself or herself in social situations will be asked to attend gatherings and speak with others.

The rationale behind exposure therapy is that by practising exposure to their fears, people have the opportunity to learn that their fears are excessive and irrational, and that the anxiety decreases with more and more practice. This process is called *habituation*.

Because many people find it hard to face their fears, exposure therapy typically starts with exposing the person to situations that create only mild to moderate symptoms of anxiety, and gradually progresses to exposing the person to situations that create severe anxiety. In the case of someone who fears dogs, therapy may begin with the person discussing dogs, then progress to the person looking at photos of dogs, watching movies that showcase dogs and watching dogs from a distance, until eventually he or she can approach and pat different types of dogs.

Again, with repeated exposure, these situations begin to elicit less and less fear and anxiety for the person, and he or she feels less of an urge to avoid them. As the person makes progress in conducting exposures with the assistance of the therapist, he or she is increasingly requested to complete exposure tasks as part of homework between sessions. The time it takes for people to progress in treatment may depend on the severity of their fear and their ability to tolerate the discomfort associated with arousing their anxiety.

An important part of CBT is helping people with anxiety disorders to identify, question and correct their tendencies to overestimate danger and their perceived inability to cope with danger. Cognitive strategies are developed in combination with exposure therapy to help people recognize that their thoughts, attitudes, beliefs and appraisals can generate and maintain anxious states.

For example, people who fear dogs may have the mistaken belief that all dogs are dangerous, based on an earlier experience with a single dog bite, and people experiencing panic attacks are likely to overestimate the likelihood of, or the threat associated with, having another panic attack in the mall. People with social phobia tend to overestimate the degree to which they are going to make social blunders and subsequently be judged and ridiculed.

With repeated practice in therapy and then as part of homework, people with anxiety disorders develop skills that enable them to identify anxiety-related thoughts and beliefs, identify common distortions in their thinking, examine the evidence that supports and does not support their fearful appraisals, and develop less-threatening alternative responses to the feared object or situation.

Cognitive restructuring exercises are also introduced to help the person recognize why behavioural avoidance, reassurance-seeking behaviours and "safety" behaviours (e.g., carrying anti-anxiety medication at all times, "just in case") are unhelpful long-term strategies.

CBT has been found to be effective for all the anxiety disorders. Most people experience a significant reduction in their symptoms and stay well after the treatment ends. Given the success of this therapy and its ability to reduce relapse, CBT is established as the first-choice psychological treatment for anxiety disorders. CBT should be offered to all people with anxiety disorders, except for those who have already completed a course of CBT and failed to improve, those who do not want to try CBT, or people who cannot access a well-trained CBT therapist. Step-by-step workbooks are available for each anxiety disorder. (See the Suggested Reading list on page 47 for recommended titles.)

Medication options

Research has shown that people with anxiety disorders often benefit from medications that affect various neurotransmitters, particularly serotonin, norepinephrine and GABA. Medications can help reduce symptoms of anxiety, especially when combined with CBT.

The main medications used to treat anxiety are selective serotonin reuptake inhibitors (SSRIs), serotonin and norepinephrine reuptake inhibitors (SNRIs) and benzodiazepines (BZDs). SSRIs and SNRIs belong to a class of drugs called antidepressants, which are commonly prescribed to treat both anxiety disorders and depression.

Doctors treating anxiety disorders will usually prescribe an SSRI or an SNRI. Research indicates that these medications help reduce the symptoms of anxiety for about 70 per cent of the people who take them. For those who do not benefit from taking an SSRI or SNRI, other drug treatments can provide relief. In some cases, specific symptoms of anxiety may be addressed with other medications, such as "beta blockers" to reduce hand tremors or slow down the heart rate, or "anticholinergics" to reduce sweating.

Such medications can be taken in addition to an SSRI or SNRI.

ANTIDEPRESSANTS

Antidepressants are usually the first medication prescribed to treat anxiety disorders. These medications are safe, effective and non-addictive, and have not been shown to have any long-term effects. The drawback of antidepressants is that they often have side-effects. For most people, the side-effects are mild and short-lived, an easy trade-off for the benefits of the medication. For others, the side-effects might be more troubling. People often experience the side-effects of an antidepressant within the first few weeks of treatment, before experiencing its benefits.

While SSRIS and SNRIS are the most commonly prescribed antidepressants in the treatment of anxiety disorders, other classes of antidepressants are also effective. These include tricyclic and tetracyclic antidepressants (TCAS) and monoamine oxidase inhibitors (MAOIS). Newer antidepressants are also available, but their effectiveness in treating anxiety disorders has not yet been established.

What's involved in trying antidepressants?

For best results, antidepressants should be taken regularly, generally once or twice each day. These and all medications should be taken only as prescribed. Taking more or less than the prescribed amount can prevent medications from working, and may even worsen some symptoms. Most doctors recommend starting at a low dose and then, if the person tolerates the medication well, slowly increasing the dose until the ideal dose is found. The ideal dose is one that provides the greatest benefit with minimum side-effects.

Once a person has begun taking an antidepressant, he or she should continue for a trial period of at least three months. This allows time for the dosage to be adjusted correctly, for the initial side-effects to subside, and for the benefits of the drug to become clear. When these drugs work, the effects come on gradually.

Usually several weeks pass before any change in symptoms is noticed. Then, the anxiety is reduced and it is easier for people to work on changing the way they behave in response to anxiety. It is important to realize that although these medications can be of great help to some people, not all symptoms of anxiety will be relieved.

If no benefits are derived from a particular antidepressant after a trial period of three months, doctors often recommend that another antidepressant be tried. Some people respond well to one drug and not at all to another. If a person does not benefit from the first medication (e.g., an SSRI), a second choice would be another SSRI or an SNRI. It is not uncommon for someone to try two or three antidepressant drugs before finding the one that works best.

The question of whether or not to take an antidepressant while pregnant or nursing should be discussed with your doctor. In some cases, the benefit of the drug clearly outweighs the possible risks.

How long should I take an antidepressant?
When the right antidepressant has been found, doctors usually advise taking the medication for at least six to 12 months. In some cases, the doctor may recommend taking the medication for several years, as there might be a greater risk of relapse if the medication is stopped. Even when taken for the long term, these medications are safe and non-addictive.

If a person begins to feel better and stops taking medication too soon or too quickly, the risk of relapse increases. The decision to stop taking medication should only be made in consultation with a doctor. The following guidelines can help lower the risk of relapse when a person wants to discontinue using medication:

· Lower the dosage gradually by "tapering," or reducing, the medication over a period of time, possibly several weeks to months.
· Follow up regularly with a health care professional to help monitor the severity of any recurring symptoms of anxiety.
· Combine CBT with medication and use the skills learned to control any symptoms of anxiety that may arise when medication is discontinued.

Side-effects of antidepressants

People who take antidepressants are likely to experience side-effects. Side-effects often begin soon after the person starts treatment, and generally diminish over time. In the early stages of treatment, side-effects may resemble anxiety symptoms, causing some people with anxiety disorders to abandon the treatment before it has had a chance to take full effect. Such side-effects, however, usually only last a couple of weeks. Some side-effects may be reduced by adjusting the dose, or by taking the medication at a different time of the day. If this approach does not improve the side-effects, the doctor may prescribe another medication.

The side-effects of antidepressants are not permanent and will disappear completely when the medication is discontinued. When taking antidepressants or any medication, it is important to discuss with your doctor any side-effects that are troubling you. Each class of antidepressant and its common side-effects are discussed below.

Drug interactions with antidepressants

When taking an antidepressant, or any medication, it is important to check with your doctor or pharmacist for possible drug interactions

before taking any other prescription or over-the-counter drugs,
or any herbal products. Check also with your doctor before using
alcohol or illegal drugs, as these may also interact with certain
medications or reduce the effectiveness of treatment.

Even on their own, alcohol and illegal drugs can create symptoms
of anxiety.

Selective serotonin reuptake inhibitors

SSRIs are often the first medication prescribed to treat anxiety
disorders. These medications are known to reduce symptoms of
anxiety, to be safe, and to have milder side-effects than some other
antidepressants. ssris have their primary effect on serotonin neurotransmitters.

The ssris currently available in Canada are: fluoxetine (Prozac),
fluvoxamine (Luvox), sertraline (Zoloft), paroxetine (Paxil), cita-
lopram (Celexa) and escitalopram (Cipralex). These medications
are considered to be equally effective, although each may work for
some people and not for others. They work less rapidly than benzodiazepines, especially in panic disorder, but are better tolerated in
the long term and do not cause physiological dependence.

Common side-effects: sexual inhibition, gastrointestinal complaints,
weight gain, headaches, anxiety, insomnia or sedation, vivid
dreams or nightmares. Some studies suggest a small increase in
the risk of suicidal behaviour in the early stages of ssri treatment.
Contact your doctor right away if this happens, and go to the
nearest emergency department immediately if you feel you are in
danger of harming yourself.

Serotonin and norepinephrine reuptake inhibitors

Venlafaxine (Effexor) is used to treat depression and generalized
anxiety disorder, and also panic disorder, ocd and social phobia.

The only other medication in this class currently available in Canada is duloxetine (Cymbalta).

Common side-effects: nausea, drowsiness, dizziness, nervousness or anxiety, fatigue, loss of appetite and sexual dysfunction; in higher dosage, venlafaxine may increase blood pressure, and should only be taken on a doctor's advice by people with hypertension or liver disease.

Tricyclic and tetracyclic antidepressants
Although there are 10 TCAs available in Canada, not all of them have been shown to be effective for the treatment of anxiety disorders. Imipramine (Tofranil), desipramine (Norpramin) and clomipramine (Anafranil) have been the most studied for the treatment of panic disorder and generalized anxiety disorder.

TCAs may interfere with certain medications, especially other mental health or heart medications. Review with your doctor the medications you are currently taking to check for possible interactions.

Common side-effects: dry mouth, tremors, constipation, sedation, blurred vision and change of blood pressure when moving from a sitting to a standing position (orthostatic hypotension). Because TCAs may cause heart rhythm abnormalities, your doctor may order an electrocardiogram (ECG), and/or other tests before prescribing this medication to you, and during the course of treatment.

Monoamine oxidase inhibitors
MAOIs are highly effective medications for the treatment of depression and anxiety. However, MAOIs are used less frequently than other antidepressants because people who take them must follow a diet that is low in tyramine, a protein found in, for example, foods that are aged, fermented or high in yeast. If tyramine is consumed in a too large a quantity while taking an MAOI, it can cause severe

high blood pressure, which may be life-threatening. If you are taking an MAOI, your doctor or pharmacist will provide you with a list of foods to avoid. Examples of MAOIS are phenelzine (Nardil) and tranylcypromine (Parnate).

MAOIs also interact with a number of medications. Some painkillers, for example, should be avoided. Ask your doctor or pharmacist for a list of medications to avoid. If you plan to have surgery, let your dentist or surgeon know you are taking an MAOI at least a few weeks before the scheduled date. You may be asked to discontinue the MAOI prior to the surgery to avoid possible drug interactions. If you require emergency surgery, your doctor will monitor and manage any possible drug interactions during and after the surgery.

Common side-effects: change of blood pressure when moving from a sitting to a standing position (orthostatic hypotension), insomnia, swelling and weight gain.

Other antidepressants
Moclobemide (Manerix) is an antidepressant related to the MAOIS, but which does not require as strict diet restrictions if taken two hours after meals, and has fewer drug interactions, making it safer than MAOIS. It is used to treat social anxiety disorder. Mirtazapine (Remeron) is an antidepressant that may also be used in the treatment of anxiety disorders, and can help with sleep and stimulate appetite at lower doses.

BENZODIAZEPINES

Benzodiazepines are a group of medications that increase the activity of the GABA neurotransmitter system. BZDS reduce anxiety and excessive excitement, and make people feel quiet and calm. They also produce drowsiness, making it easier to fall asleep and to sleep through the night. For a long time, before SSRIS were available,

BZDS were the drugs of choice for managing anxiety disorders. However, these drugs have potential for abuse and can be addictive, so the long-term use of BZDS is discouraged.

BZDs are often used to treat generalized anxiety disorder, panic disorder and social anxiety disorder. They are usually prescribed in addition to an SSRI or other antidepressant for two to four weeks at the beginning of treatment, until the antidepressant becomes fully effective. The advantage of BZDS is that they can rapidly relieve and control anxiety.

The BZDS most commonly used to treat anxiety disorders are clonazepam (Rivotril)and lorazepam (Ativan).

Common side-effects: drowsiness, sedation, dizziness and loss of balance; effects are most serious when BZDS are combined with alcohol or with other sedative medications.

OTHER MEDICATIONS

Buspirone (Buspar) can be used to treat generalized anxiety disorder. It works mainly through the serotonin neurotransmitter system and usually takes two to three weeks to become effective.

Antipsychotic medications are sometimes used to treat anxiety disorders. When prescribed, they are generally given at a low dose, and sometimes in combination with antidepressants to people with severe anxiety who do not respond to antidepressants alone.

HERBAL THERAPIES

Over the years, many herbs have been thought to have some effect on mood and mental health. Although many plants may have active ingredients that can be somewhat effective in relieving various symptoms, their effectiveness has not been formally tested. In North America, the herbal industry is unregulated, meaning that the quality and effectiveness of herbal products is not consistent. Adverse effects are possible, as are toxic interactions with other drugs. If you are considering herbal medicines, you should discuss this with your doctor and review the medications you are already taking.

Some herbal products have sedative effects and are believed to reduce symptoms of anxiety. These include German chamomile, hops, kava kava, lemon balm, passion flower, skullcap and valerian. Other herbs without sedating effects, such as St. John's wort, have also been suggested for treating anxiety disorders. Very little research has been done to determine the effectiveness of these herbal therapies, either as stand-alone treatment or in combination with well-established treatments, such as CBT and antidepressant medications.

Other therapeutic options

EXERCISE

The relationship between physical activity and emotional well-being has been known for some time. Research on exercise in the context of anxiety treatment is still in the early stages; however, the research that has been done suggests that exercise tailored to a person's physical health and fitness levels is a promising addition to psychological or medication treatment of anxiety.

MINDFULNESS

Mindfulness-based cognitive therapy (MBCT) combines CBT strategies with mindfulness meditation. Through daily meditation practice, people's tolerance and acceptance of their present-moment experience is increased, and their judgement of their experience is decreased. An aim of MBCT is for people to change their relationship with their own experience. This differs from the focus of standard CBT (without mindfulness), which is to decrease the anxiety experience itself by changing upsetting thoughts and behaviours.

MBCT is a popular therapeutic option for emotional difficulties. It is currently recommended for preventing relapse of depression in people who have previously been depressed. Studies looking at the effectiveness of MBCT as a treatment for anxiety disorders suggest that it reduces symptoms of anxiety, particularly for people with social anxiety disorder. The few studies that have compared MBCT to CBT for individuals with social anxiety disorder suggest that MBCT is as effective as or is less effective than CBT. MBCT has not been shown to be as effective as CBT for those with GAD. However, more research is needed to confirm the effectiveness of mindfulness as a treatment for anxiety disorders. A related treatment is mindfulness-based stress reduction (MBSR), which does not have the cognitive component, and appears to be less effective than MBCT for anxiety.

MBCT is not a disorder-specific treatment, and it likely addresses a range of contributors to general well-being (e.g., self-criticism). MBCT is typically delivered over eight weeks in a group format, although it can also be done in an individual format.

ACCEPTANCE AND COMMITMENT THERAPY
Acceptance and commitment therapy (ACT) aims to increase psychological flexibility through six change processes: acceptance, cognitive fusion, being present, self as context, values and committed action. Research into the effectiveness of ACT as a treatment for anxiety disorders shows that it is not more effective than CBT; however, it has been shown to be more effective than no treatment

for general anxiety disorder and social phobia. More research is needed to determine the effectiveness of ACT, compared to no treatment, for specific phobias and panic. When CBT is declined or when more help is needed, ACT could be added.

4 Recovery and relapse prevention

When someone begins treatment for an anxiety disorder, the first goal is to reduce and manage symptoms. The process of achieving this goal, known as "recovery," often includes a combination of medication, CBT and supportive psychotherapy, and may also include other support such as occupational, recreation and nutrition therapy. Recovery also includes the way you apply the skills learned in treatment to real-life situations. Your idea of what you hope to achieve through recovery is unique to you. Long-term goals may include improved relationships with others, a full and satisfying work life, increased self-esteem and improved overall quality of life.

Once recovery is underway, and you are ready to focus on getting your life back to normal, the next step is "relapse prevention." Anxiety is not an illness with a "cure." Medication and therapy can help to bring symptoms under control, but some of the symptoms of anxiety, such as worry and fear, can arise for anyone during everyday life. To prevent relapse, you need to be ready with a plan to manage symptoms as they appear. Moving through the process of recovery and relapse prevention depends on a combination of planning and attitude. Achieving and maintaining your goals is easier when you develop:

· awareness of warning signs and strategies to respond to setbacks
· a healthy lifestyle

· hope and optimism about the future
· self-confidence.

Preventing relapse and promoting wellness

SOME THINGS YOU CAN DO TO PREVENT RELAPSE

1. **Become an expert on your condition.** Learn about your symptoms and how to recognize when symptoms begin. Many resources are available, including books, videos, support groups and information on the Internet. Be aware that not all Internet sites provide reliable information; see the resources section beginning on page 47, for recommended sites and other suggestions for further information.

2. **Develop and stick to a plan for managing symptoms of anxiety.** Maintaining improvements in symptoms of anxiety requires commitment and dedication. Resist the urge to limit your life in the same way that you did when you were in the grips of your anxiety disorder. Develop a plan that includes a commitment to:
   - Take medications as prescribed. Any changes in your medication routine should be discussed beforehand with your doctor.
   - Learn warning signs that the anxiety disorder could be returning (e.g., if you begin again to avoid situations you previously associated with anxiety).
   - Respond to warning signs by using the skills learned during therapy. To remain well, continue to expose yourself to situations you associated with anxiety.

3. **Develop a social support network**. Family, friends and a support group can help you to recognize when stressful situations may trigger anxiety symptoms, and can remind you of your strengths when you feel discouraged.

4. **Learn to cope with stress**. Stress, fatigue and feeling out of control can trigger symptoms of anxiety. Pay attention to which situations are stressful for you. Learn ways to manage stress. Here are some suggestions that can help you to return to a calm state:

   - *Diaphragmatic breathing*: One way to do this is to lie on your back with one hand over your navel. Breathe so that your hand rises and falls with each breath, allowing your lungs to completely empty and fill. Ask your clinician about other approaches to this technique.

   - *Pleasurable activities*: Do something you enjoy that is relaxing, such as reading an inspiring book, walking in nature or talking to a supportive person.

   - *Take action*: When you take your mind off the things that cause you stress, it can make them seem less important. Take a class or try a new interest; learn something new.

   - *Become more aware of the present moment*: Yoga and mindfulness meditation are two ways to help you focus your mind on the here and now.

5. **Live a healthy life**. Eat a healthy diet, sleep well and exercise. Regular exercise, including sports, can help to manage stress. If you choose to drink alcohol, use it in moderation. Use your faith, religion or spiritual practices to support your recovery. Remain connected with the aspects of life that nurture you, and explore new ways to nurture yourself.

6. **Focus on developing a well-balanced life**, with time for work, family, friends and leisure activities.

Relationship with a partner

An anxiety disorder can affect your relationship with your partner. When your symptoms are severe, it may be hard for you to be supportive and intimate. When you are most affected by your anxiety disorder, your partner may take on more responsibilities than he or she feels is fair. Over time, this can lead to distance and even hostility in the relationship. It takes time, patience and effort to rebuild what may have been lost.

Include your partner in your recovery. Let him or her know about your progress, and begin to offer to take on more responsibility again as you make improvements in managing your symptoms. It may be helpful for your partner to meet with your clinician, to better understand your treatment. Your partner may benefit from a family support group as well.

Couple therapy with a marital or couple therapist who understands anxiety disorders can help you to improve communication and to work together as a couple once again. A good therapist can help to remind couples of what brought them together in the first place.

5 Help for families and friends

What happens when someone you love has an anxiety disorder?

When someone in the family has an anxiety disorder, it affects everyone and brings added pressures. Because most people experience some degree of anxiety in life, it may be quite some time before your relative receives an accurate diagnosis and begins to receive treatment. They may have heard well-meaning advice, like, "You worry too much. Relax." Or, "What's the problem with going out of the house? Just do it!" You may even have said these things to them. To a person without an anxiety disorder, these statements would be good advice, but having an anxiety disorder involves more than the usual worry. Your relative may require professional help to get well.

It is natural for families and partners to feel resentful or disappointed when anxiety interferes with normal family life. Acknowledging the illness can be the first step toward understanding and making the family work again.

When your relative is first diagnosed

When a member of your family is diagnosed with an anxiety disorder, you may experience varied and conflicting emotions. Often when a family learns that an anxiety disorder is the cause of their relative's worry and behaviour, they feel relief to finally know what the problem is, but they may also feel uncomfortable emotions, such as sadness, fear, guilt or anger. You may fear how the illness will affect the future for your relative, and for you. If you are the parent of a child or young adult who has been diagnosed with an anxiety disorder, you may feel guilty and blame yourself for the illness. You may fear that you have done something to bring this on, even when health care professionals tell you that this is not the case. Not surprisingly, you may feel angry that an anxiety disorder has disrupted the life of your family.

It is normal to experience this wide range of feelings. Understanding this, and learning to accept and manage your feelings, will reduce your stress and help you to be more helpful to the person who is struggling with the anxiety disorder.

How to relate to your family member

1. **Learn as much as you can about the symptoms of and treatments for your relative's anxiety disorder.** This will help you understand and support your relative as he or she makes changes.

2. **Encourage your family member to follow the treatment plan.** If you have questions about your relative's treatment, ask your relative if it would be possible to speak to a member of his or her treatment team.

3. **Try to keep anxiety from taking over family life.** Keep stress low and family life normal as much as possible.

4. **Be supportive of your relative, without supporting his or her anxiety.** Your relative or friend may look to you for reassurance when he or she is anxious, or ask you to arrange things to help him or her avoid an anxiety-producing situation. If you have helped your relative to reduce or avoid anxiety in the past, it may take time and practice to change this pattern. When you resist supporting your relative's anxiety behaviours, (e.g., avoiding anxiety-provoking situations, blocking feelings of anxiety with excessive behaviours such as over-preparing or over-researching), you are supporting his or her efforts to get well.

5. **Communicate with your relative or friend positively, directly and clearly.** You may see things differently from your relative or friend, who may become overwhelmed by fears. Avoid personal criticism even when disagreeing. For example, if your relative does not wish to seek treatment at the time that you think it is needed, take time to listen to his or her concerns. Express your point of view, while respecting your relative's concerns.

6. **Remember that life is a marathon, not a sprint.** Progress is made in small steps. Applaud your relative's progress at confronting anxiety and encourage him or her to use skills learned in treatment to manage symptoms.

Taking care of yourself

When family members, partners or friends are caught up in caring for a relative with an anxiety disorder, they may neglect to take care of themselves. At times they may give up their own activities and become isolated from friends and colleagues. The isolation could go on for some time before they realize how emotionally and physically drained they are from caring for their relative or partner. The stress can result in disturbed sleeping patterns, feelings of irritability and/or episodes of exhaustion.

Family and friend caregivers or partners need to be aware of their personal signs of stress and know their personal limits. They need to take actions to maintain their physical and mental health. Taking time out for oneself and keeping up interests outside of the family, and apart from the relative with an anxiety disorder, can help the family caregiver to recharge. Recovery from an anxiety disorder can be a long process. Caregivers need to set aside feelings of guilt, or of pressure to focus always on the relative who needs help. When caregivers take the time to have their own needs met, they have more energy and patience to support their relative, and are less likely to feel resentful or overwhelmed.

Family and friends can offer valuable support. However, when seeking such support, it is important to be aware that some people are more informed and understanding about mental health problems than others. It is wise to be selective when choosing who to confide in, and what advice to follow.

Family caregivers are encouraged to seek professional support that is specific to families of people with mental health problems. Support could include individual or family counselling, family support and education groups to improve understanding of their relative's anxiety disorder, and self-help groups where families of people with anxiety disorders provide support to each other.

Counselling and groups may be offered by a community hospital, clinic or mental health organization.

Explaining anxiety disorders to children

It can be challenging to explain anxiety disorders to children. Sometimes parents will not tell their children that a family member has been diagnosed with an anxiety disorder because they do not know how to explain it to children or they think children will not understand. In an effort to protect children, they sometimes continue with family routines as if nothing was wrong.

The strategies of saying nothing and continuing with routine activities are difficult to maintain, and over time will only be confusing to children trying to understand their relative's problem. Because children are sensitive and intuitive they will notice when a member of the family has emotional, mental and physical changes. Parents should avoid being secretive about the relative's anxiety disorder, as children will develop their own—often wrong—ideas about their relative's condition.

Children from three to seven years of age tend to see the world as revolving around them. As a consequence they blame themselves for unusual and upsetting events or changes in the family, or for unusual changes that occur with other people. For example, if a member of the family has a fear of heights, and becomes upset when a child climbs a ladder, the child may assume he or she is the cause of the person's unusual behaviour.

To explain anxiety disorders to children, it is important to provide them with only as much information as they are mature or old enough to understand. When providing information to toddlers and preschool children, parents should use simple, short sentences. That is, the sentences should be worded in concrete language and be free of technical information. For example, "Sometimes your father doesn't feel well and it makes him upset." Or, "Your father has an illness that makes him feel upset when he sees someone climb a ladder."

Children in elementary school can process more information. They are more able to understand the concept of an anxiety disorder as an illness; however, too much detail about the nature of the illness and how it is being treated could overwhelm them. One way to explain anxiety disorders to elementary school children is to say, "An anxiety disorder is a kind of illness that makes people worry a lot about heights and getting sick. Worrying so much makes them avoid tall buildings."

Teenagers can manage most information, and often need to talk about what they see and feel. They may worry about the stigma of mental health problems and may ask about the genetics of anxiety disorders. Teenagers will engage in conversations about anxiety disorders if information is shared with them.

There are three main areas that are helpful for parents to cover when speaking with children about anxiety disorders:

1. **The parent or family member behaves this way because he or she has an illness.** It is easiest for children to understand an anxiety disorder when it is explained to them as an illness. Tell children that a member of the family has an illness called an anxiety disorder. You may explain it like this: "An anxiety disorder is like a cold, except that you don't catch it, and rather than giving you a runny nose, it makes you worry a lot, sometimes for no reason. This worry makes people with an anxiety disorder avoid heights, or stay away from things that bother them. Sometimes, they want others in the family to act the same way that they do. An anxiety disorder takes a long time to get better. People with an anxiety disorder need help from a doctor or therapist."

2. **Reassure the child that he or she did not make the parent or family member get this illness.** Children need to know that their actions did not cause their loved one to develop the illness. People with anxiety disorders may become depressed as they struggle with their symptoms. It is important to reassure children that they did not make their loved one fearful or anxious.

3. **Reassure the child that the adults in the family and other people, such as doctors, are trying to help the affected person.** It is the responsibility of adults to take care of the family member with an anxiety disorder. Children should not worry about taking care of anyone who is ill. Children need their parents and other trusted adults to protect them. Children should be allowed to talk about what they see and feel with someone who knows how hard it is for a relative to struggle with the symptoms of an anxiety disorder. The changes that occur in a loved one because of an anxiety disorder are often scary to children. They miss the time spent with the person who is ill.

Participating in activities outside the home helps children as it exposes them to healthy relationships. As the relative with an anxiety disorder recovers, and he or she gradually resumes family activities, this will help to improve his or her relationship with the children in the family.

If the relative with an anxiety disorder is a parent, he or she and the other parent should talk with the children about explaining the anxiety disorder to people outside the family. The support of friends is important for everyone. However, because anxiety disorders can be hard to explain, and some families worry about the stigma of mental illness, family members will have to decide how open they wish to be about their situation.

Some parents who are affected with an anxiety disorder may find that they are less patient and more easily irritated than usual.

They may find it hard to tolerate the loud, messy, chaotic play of their children. For them, the family may have to design and develop structured routines to ensure that the parent with an anxiety disorder has quiet and restful time away from situations that might trigger symptoms of the illness. Times should be planned to allow for children to play outside the home, or for the parent with an anxiety disorder to rest for part of the day in a quiet area of the home.

When the relative with an anxiety disorder is in recovery, it helps for the person to explain his or her behaviour to the children. The recovered relative may need to plan some special times with the children to re-establish their relationship and reassure the children that he or she is now more available to them.

Reference

American Psychiatric Association. (2013). *Diagnostic and Statistical Manual of Mental Disorders* (5th ed.), Washington, DC: Author.

Resources

SUGGESTED READING

General anxiety, stress and depression

Abramowitz, J.S. (2012). *The Stress Less Workbook: Simple Strategies to Relieve Pressure, Manage Commitments, and Minimize Conflicts.* New York: Guilford Press.

Antony, M.M. & Norton, P.J. (2008). *The Anti-Anxiety Workbook: Proven Strategies to Overcome Worry, Panic, Phobias, and Obsessions.* New York: Guilford Press.

Bieling, P.J. & Antony, M.M. (2003). *Ending the Depression Cycle: A Step-by-Step Guide for Preventing Relapse.* Oakland, CA: New Harbinger Publications.

Bourne, E.J. (2015). *The Anxiety & Phobia Workbook* (6th ed.). Oakland, CA: New Harbinger Publications.

Burns, D.D. (2008). *Feeling Good: A New Mood Therapy* (revised and updated). New York: HarperCollins.

Clark, D.A. & Beck, A.T. (2012). *The Anxiety and Worry Workbook: The Cognitive Behavioral Solution.* New York: Guilford Press.

Davis, M., Eshelman, E.R. & McKay, M. (2008). *The Relaxation and Stress Reduction Workbook* (6th ed.). Oakland, CA: New Harbinger Publications.

Forsyth, J.P. & Eifert, G.H. (2007). *The Mindfulness and Acceptance Workbook for Anxiety: A Guide to Breaking Free from Anxiety, Phobias, and Worry Using Acceptance and Commitment Therapy.* Oakland, CA: New Harbinger Publications.

Greenberger, D. & Padesky, C.A. (2015). *Mind over Mood: Change How You Feel by Changing the Way You Think* (2nd ed.). New York: Guilford Press.

Orsillo, S.M. & Roemer, L. (2011). *A Mindful Way through Anxiety: Break Free from Chronic Worry and Reclaim Your Life.* New York: Guilford Press.

Otto, M.W. & Smits, J.A.J. (2009). *Exercise for Mood and Anxiety Disorders: Workbook.* New York: Oxford University Press.

Otto, M.W. & Smits, J.A.J. (2011). *Exercise for Mood and Anxiety Disorders: Proven Strategies for Overcoming Depression and Enhancing Well-Being.* New York: Oxford University Press.

Williams, M., Teasdale, J. & Segal, Z. (2007). *The Mindful Way through Depression.* New York: Guilford Press.

Wright, J.H. & McCray, L.W. (2012). *Breaking Free from Depression: Pathways to Wellness.* New York: Guilford Press.

Generalized anxiety disorder
Craske, M. & Barlow, D. (2006). *Mastery of Your Anxiety and Worry: Workbook* (2nd ed.). New York: Oxford University Press.

Gyoerkoe, K.L. & Wiegartz, P.S. (2006). *10 Simple Solutions to Worry: How to Calm Your Mind, Relax Your Body, & Reclaim Your Life*. Oakland, CA: New Harbinger Publications.

Leahy, R. (2005). *The Worry Cure: Seven Steps to Stop Worry from Stopping You*. New York: Three Rivers Press.

Meares, K. & Freeston, M. (2008). *Overcoming Worry: A Self-Help Guide Using Cognitive Behavioral Techniques*. New York: Basic Books.

Robichaud, M. & Dugas, M.J. (2015). *The Generalized Anxiety Disorder Workbook: A Comprehensive CBT Guide for Coping with Uncertainty, Worry, and Fear*. Oakland, CA: New Harbinger.

Panic disorder

Antony, M.M. & McCabe, R.E. (2004). *10 Simple Solutions to Panic: How to Overcome Panic Attacks, Calm Physical Symptoms, and Reclaim Your Life*. Oakland, CA: New Harbinger Publications.

Barlow, D.H. & Craske, M.G. (2006). *Mastery of Your Anxiety and Panic: Workbook* (4th ed.). New York: Oxford University Press.

Wilson, R. (2009). *Don't Panic: Taking Control of Anxiety Attacks* (3rd ed.). New York: HarperCollins.

Social anxiety disorder

Antony, M.M. & Swinson, R.P. (2008). *The Shyness and Social Anxiety Workbook: Proven Step-by-Step Techniques for Overcoming Your Fear* (2nd ed.). Oakland, CA: New Harbinger Publications.

Hope, D.A., Heimberg, R.G. & Turk, C.L. (2010). *Managing Social Anxiety: A Cognitive Behavioral Therapy Approach: Workbook* (2nd ed.). New York: Oxford University Press.

Stein, M.B. & Walker, J.R. (2009). *Triumph over Shyness: Conquering Social Anxiety Disorder (2nd ed.)*. Silver Spring, MD: Anxiety Disorders Association of America.

Specific phobia

Antony, M.M., Craske, M.G. & Barlow, D.H. (2006). *Mastering Your Fears and Phobias: Workbook* (2nd ed.). New York: Oxford University Press.

Internet resources

American Psychological Association
www.apa.org

Canadian Psychological Association
www.cpa.ca/

Anxiety Disorders Association of America
www.adaa.org

Association for Behavioral and Cognitive Therapies
www.abct.org

Canadian Association of Cognitive and Behavioural Therapies
www.cacbt.ca

Canadian Mental Health Association
www.cmha.ca

Other guides in this series

Addiction

Bipolar Disorder

Cognitive-Behavioural Therapy

Concurrent Substance Use and Mental Health Disorders

Depression

Dual Diagnosis

First Episode Psychosis

The Forensic Mental Health System in Ontario

Obsessive-Compulsive Disorder

Schizophrenia

Women, Abuse and Trauma Therapy

Women and Psychosis

This publication may be available in other formats. For information about alternative formats or other CAMH publications, or to place an order, please contact CAMH Publications:

Toll-free: 1 800 661-1111
Toronto: 416 595-6059
E-mail: publications@camh.ca
Online store: http://store.camh.ca